Wilderness Survival Guide for Kids

How to Perform First aid, Build a Fire, Build Shelter and Everything you need to know about Surviving Outdoors

Jason Benntle

Copyright 2021 © Jason Benntle
All rights reserved. This book is copyright, and no part of it may be reproduced, stored, or transmitted, in any form or means, without the prior written permission of the copyright owner.
Printed in the United States of America.
Copyright 2021 © Jason Benntle

Table of Contents

- INTRODUCTION 5
- UNDERSTANDING THE WILDERNESS: NURTURING A CONNECTION WITH NATURE 5
- CHAPTER ONE 9
- PREPARING FOR OUTDOOR ADVENTURES: EQUIPPING KIDS FOR WILDERNESS EXPLORATION 9
- CHAPTER TWO 15
- BASIC FIRST AID FOR KIDS: EMPOWERING YOUNG EXPLORERS WITH LIFE-SAVING SKILLS 15
- CHAPTER THREE 23
- FINDING WATER SOURCES: NAVIGATING HYDRATION IN THE WILDERNESS 23
- CHAPTER FOUR 29
- BUILDING A FIRE: IGNITING ESSENTIAL WILDERNESS SKILLS IN KIDS 29
- CHAPTER FIVE 39
- CONSTRUCTING A SHELTER: CRAFTING WILDERNESS REFUGES FOR KIDS 39

CHAPTER SIX 47

NAVIGATION IN THE WILDERNESS: NAVIGATING THE WILD WITH CONFIDENCE 47

CHAPTER SEVEN 57

IDENTIFYING EDIBLE PLANTS AND WILDLIFE: NOURISHMENT FROM NATURE IN WILDERNESS SURVIVAL FOR KIDS 57

CHAPTER EIGHT 69

SURVIVAL GAMES AND DRILLS FOR KIDS: FOSTERING SKILLS, CONFIDENCE, AND FUN IN THE WILDERNESS 69

CHAPTER NINE 80

EMERGENCY SITUATIONS AND CALLING FOR HELP: EMPOWERING KIDS WITH LIFESAVING SKILLS 80

INTRODUCTION

UNDERSTANDING THE WILDERNESS: NURTURING A CONNECTION WITH NATURE

The wilderness is a vast and untamed expanse, offering both beauty and challenges to those who venture into its embrace. For kids, developing an understanding of the wilderness goes beyond merely recognizing trees and animals; it's about fostering a profound connection with nature and learning how to coexist harmoniously. In this section, we delve into the importance of wilderness survival for children and introduce them to the fundamental principles that will guide their outdoor adventures.

Importance of Wilderness Survival for Kids

Engaging with the wilderness provides children with a myriad of benefits, ranging from physical fitness to cognitive development. Beyond the obvious advantages, such as fresh air and exercise, spending time in nature enhances a child's ability to problem-solve, increases attention span, and promotes creativity.

Wilderness survival skills, specifically tailored for kids, instill a sense of confidence and self-reliance. As they learn to navigate challenges in the wild, children develop resilience, adaptability, and a deeper appreciation for their surroundings. The sense of accomplishment gained from building a shelter or starting a fire can boost self-esteem and foster a lifelong love for outdoor activities.

Moreover, connecting with nature at a young age nurtures environmental stewardship. Kids who understand the delicate balance of ecosystems and the importance of preserving wilderness areas are more likely to become responsible and environmentally conscious adults. Teaching them the principles of Leave No Trace ensures that they appreciate the impact of their actions on the environment and strive to minimize it.

Basic Principles for Kids

Before embarking on any outdoor adventure, children must grasp some fundamental principles that will guide their interactions with the wilderness. These principles lay the foundation for responsible and safe exploration

- **Respect for Nature:** Teach kids the importance of treating nature with respect. This involves not disturbing plants and animals, staying on designated trails, and minimizing their impact on the environment.

- **Preparation and Planning:** Instill the value of preparation in kids. This includes checking the weather forecast, informing someone of the trip plans, and carrying the necessary gear and supplies. Planning ahead ensures a safer and more enjoyable outdoor experience.

- **Safety First**: Impress upon children the significance of prioritizing safety. From using proper gear to following safety guidelines, emphasizing the importance of precautionary measures will help them develop a safety-conscious mindset.

- **Leave No Trace:** Introduce the Leave No Trace principles, emphasizing the importance of leaving nature as they found it. This includes packing out all trash, respecting wildlife from a distance, and avoiding unnecessary impact on the ecosystem.

- **Awareness and Observation:** Encourage kids to be observant and aware of their surroundings. Developing keen observational skills helps them identify potential hazards, locate resources, and appreciate the beauty of nature.

- **Teamwork and Communication**: In the wilderness, teamwork is essential. Teach kids the value of working together, communicating effectively, and looking out for one another. These skills not only enhance safety but also foster a sense of camaraderie.

By imparting these basic principles to children, we equip them with the tools they need to engage with the wilderness responsibly. The aim is not only to teach survival skills but also to cultivate a lifelong appreciation for the natural world, ensuring that they become stewards of the environment as they grow older.

CHAPTER ONE

PREPARING FOR OUTDOOR ADVENTURES: EQUIPPING KIDS FOR WILDERNESS EXPLORATION

Preparation is the key to a successful and safe outdoor adventure, especially when it comes to wilderness survival for kids. In this section, we delve into the essential aspects of preparing for outdoor activities, emphasizing the importance of proper gear, thorough trip planning, and instilling safety measures that will empower children to navigate the challenges of the wilderness with confidence.

Essential Gear for Kids

Equipping children with the right gear is crucial for their safety and comfort in the wilderness. While the specific gear may vary based on the nature of the outdoor activity, certain fundamental items are essential for any expedition:

- **Clothing:** Proper attire is the first line of defense against the elements. Teach kids the importance of layering, and ensure they have appropriate clothing for the weather conditions. This includes a waterproof jacket, insulated layers, sturdy footwear, and a hat for sun protection.

- **Backpack:** A well-fitted backpack is essential for carrying gear and supplies. Opt for a size-appropriate backpack that allows kids to carry their essentials comfortably. Emphasize the importance of distributing weight evenly and adjusting straps for a secure fit.

- **Navigation Tools:** Basic navigation tools are essential for teaching kids how to find their way in the wilderness. Include a simple compass and map in their gear, and teach them how to use these tools to navigate trails and understand their surroundings.

- **First Aid Kit:** A compact and child-friendly first aid kit is a must-have for any outdoor adventure. Ensure it includes bandages, antiseptic wipes, tweezers, and any necessary personal medications. Teach kids how to use basic first aid supplies for minor injuries.

- **Water and Hydration**: Staying hydrated is critical, especially during outdoor activities. Provide kids with a reusable water bottle and emphasize the importance of regular hydration breaks. Teach them how to identify safe water sources and the importance of water purification methods.

- **Food and Snacks:** Pack nutritious and easy-to-carry snacks to keep kids energized throughout the day. Depending on the duration of the adventure, include lightweight meals that require minimal preparation. Teach them about the importance of balanced nutrition in the wilderness.

- **Emergency Supplies:** Prepare kids for unexpected situations by including emergency supplies in their gear. This may include a whistle, a flashlight with extra batteries, a space blanket, and a multipurpose tool. Teach them how to use these items responsibly and in case of emergencies.

Trip Planning and Safety Measures

Trip planning is a crucial aspect of wilderness survival, and involving kids in the process instills a sense of responsibility and awareness. The following steps outline an effective approach to trip planning for kids:

Research and Choose the Destination:

Involve children in the decision-making process by researching potential outdoor destinations together. Consider factors such as distance, terrain difficulty, and the type of activities available. Choose a destination that aligns with the group's skill level and interests.

Check Weather Conditions:

Teach kids to check the weather forecast before heading out. Discuss the potential impact of weather conditions on the trip and explain how proper clothing and gear can mitigate risks. Emphasize the importance of flexibility and being prepared for changing weather.

Inform Someone of Your Plans:

Before embarking on any outdoor adventure, inform a responsible adult or family member of your plans. Share details such as the destination, expected duration of the trip, and any specific routes or landmarks. Provide an estimated return time and contact information.

Create a Trip Itinerary:

Work with kids to create a trip itinerary that outlines the planned activities, rest breaks, and meal times. This helps set expectations and ensures a well-organized adventure. Include points of interest and potential emergency exits on the itinerary.

Safety Briefing:

Before setting out, conduct a safety briefing with the kids. Discuss potential hazards, emergency procedures, and the importance of following guidelines. Teach them how to recognize and respond to signs of distress or danger.

Buddy System:

Implement the buddy system to enhance safety. Pair kids up and emphasize the importance of sticking together. Encourage open communication between buddies and teach them to look out for each other.

Leave No Trace Principles:

Reinforce the importance of Leave No Trace principles during trip planning. Discuss responsible outdoor behavior, such as packing out trash, staying on designated trails, and minimizing impact on the environment. Instill a sense of environmental stewardship in kids from the outset.

Practice Setting Up Gear:

Before heading into the wilderness, practice setting up tents, using equipment, and organizing gear. This not only familiarizes kids with their equipment but also ensures a smoother experience in the field. Reinforce the principles of proper gear use and maintenance.

Review Basic Wilderness Skills:

Take the time to review basic wilderness survival skills with the kids. This may include demonstrating how to use a compass, build a simple shelter, and administer basic first aid. Reinforce these skills through hands-on practice to boost confidence.

By involving kids in the trip planning process and teaching them about essential gear and safety measures, we empower them to take an active role in their outdoor experiences. This hands-on approach not only imparts valuable skills but also fosters a sense of responsibility and confidence that will serve them well in the wilderness and beyond.

CHAPTER TWO

BASIC FIRST AID FOR KIDS: EMPOWERING YOUNG EXPLORERS WITH LIFE-SAVING SKILLS

Understanding basic first aid is a crucial aspect of wilderness survival for kids. In this section, we delve into the importance of teaching children first aid skills, identifying common wilderness injuries, building a basic first aid kit, and providing a step-by-step guide on administering first aid. By empowering young explorers with these life-saving skills, we equip them to handle emergencies in the outdoors responsibly.

Identifying Common Wilderness Injuries

Before delving into first aid techniques, it's essential for kids to understand the types of injuries they may encounter in the wilderness. By recognizing common injuries, they can better respond to emergencies. Key wilderness injuries include:

- **Cuts and Scrapes:** Encourage kids to wear appropriate clothing and footwear to minimize the risk of cuts and scrapes. In the event of an injury, teach them to clean the wound with antiseptic wipes, apply a sterile bandage, and elevate the injured limb if necessary.

- **Sprains and Strains:** Exploring uneven terrain increases the risk of sprains and strains. Teach kids the importance of proper footwear and how to recognize and respond to these injuries. RICE (Rest, Ice, Compression, Elevation) is a simple acronym to remember for managing these injuries.

- **Bites and Stings:** Insects, spiders, and other wildlife may pose a threat, and bites or stings can occur. Teach kids to be cautious and avoid disturbing wildlife. In the event of a bite or sting, they should clean the area, apply a cold compress, and, if necessary, take an antihistamine for allergic reactions.

- **Bruises and Minor Injuries:** While exploring, kids may encounter minor injuries such as bruises. Emphasize the importance of reporting any injuries to an adult, even if they seem minor. Teach them to apply ice to reduce swelling and to rest the injured area.

- **Burns:** Campfires and cooking activities increase the risk of burns. Stress the importance of fire safety rules and keeping a safe distance from flames. In the event of a minor burn, teach kids to cool the affected area with cold water and apply a sterile bandage.

- **Heat Exhaustion and Dehydration:** Outdoor activities can lead to heat-related illnesses. Teach kids to recognize the signs of heat exhaustion, such as excessive sweating and weakness. Emphasize the importance of staying hydrated by drinking water regularly, especially in hot weather.

Building a Basic First Aid Kit

Preparing a basic first aid kit is a practical and empowering step in teaching kids about wilderness survival. The kit should be compact, easily accessible, and tailored to address common injuries. Here's a simple guide to building a basic first aid kit for kids:

Container: Select a durable and waterproof container to hold the first aid supplies. A zippered pouch or a small plastic container with a secure lid works well.

Bandages and Dressings: Include an assortment of adhesive bandages, sterile gauze pads, and adhesive tape. These items are essential for covering cuts and wounds.

Antiseptic Wipes: Pack individually wrapped antiseptic wipes to clean wounds and prevent infection. Emphasize the importance of cleaning cuts and scrapes promptly.

Tweezers and Scissors: Include a pair of blunt-edged tweezers for removing splinters and a pair of small scissors for cutting bandages and tape.

Pain Relievers: Include child-friendly pain relievers, such as acetaminophen or ibuprofen, in pre-measured doses. Ensure that parents or guardians are aware of and approve the use of these medications.

Cold Pack: A compact instant cold pack is useful for treating minor burns, bruises, and swelling. Teach kids how to activate and use the cold pack safely.

Personal Medications: If a child requires specific medications, ensure that they are included in the first aid kit. Clearly label any medications with the child's name and dosage instructions.

Emergency Contact Information: Include a small card with emergency contact information, including names and phone numbers of parents or guardians, as well as any relevant medical information.

Instructions Manual: Include a simplified first aid instruction manual with step-by-step guidance on common injuries and how to use the items in the kit. Encourage kids to familiarize themselves with the manual.

Administering First Aid: Step-by-Step Guide

Teaching kids how to administer basic first aid is a hands-on process that enhances their confidence and preparedness. Use a step-by-step guide to walk them through common first aid scenarios:

Step 1: Assess the Situation

Before providing first aid, ensure the scene is safe. Identify potential hazards and assess the severity of the situation. Teach kids to prioritize their safety and the safety of others.

Step 2: Call for Help

In case of a serious injury or emergency, teach kids how to call for help. Emphasize the importance of remaining calm and providing clear information to emergency services.

Step 3: Approach Cautiously

Approach an injured person cautiously, introducing themselves and asking if the person needs help. Reassure the injured person and maintain a calm demeanor.

Step 4: Use Personal Protective Equipment (PPE)

Teach kids to use personal protective equipment, such as disposable gloves, when providing first aid. This helps prevent the spread of infections and ensures their safety.

Step 5: Assess the Injured Person

Encourage kids to assess the injured person's condition. Ask questions to gather information about allergies, medications, and any pre-existing conditions. This information is crucial for emergency responders.

Step 6: Control Bleeding

In the case of a cut or scrape with bleeding, teach kids to apply direct pressure using a sterile bandage or clean cloth. Elevate the injured limb if possible to help control bleeding.

Step 7: Clean and Dress Wounds

Instruct kids on how to clean wounds using antiseptic wipes and dress them with sterile bandages. Emphasize the importance of keeping the wound clean to prevent infection.

Step 8: Immobilize Injured Limbs

For sprains or fractures, teach kids how to immobilize the injured limb using a splint or by providing support with bandages. Reinforce the importance of seeking professional medical help for serious injuries.

Step 9: Comfort and Reassure

In any first aid situation, emphasize the importance of providing comfort and reassurance to the injured person. Teach kids to stay with the person until help arrives and to offer words of encouragement.

Step 10: Record and Report

Instruct kids to record details of the first aid administered, including the time, actions taken, and any changes in the person's condition. This information is valuable for medical professionals.

Step 11: Seek Professional Help

Reinforce the idea that while basic first aid is essential, seeking professional medical help is crucial for more serious injuries. Teach kids to recognize when a situation requires professional intervention.

Conclusion

By imparting basic first aid skills to children, we empower them to navigate the challenges of the wilderness responsibly. These skills not only enhance their safety during outdoor adventures but also instill a sense of confidence and self-reliance. Encouraging a hands-on approach to first aid education ensures that kids are well-prepared to handle emergencies and contribute to the well-being of their peers in the great outdoors.

CHAPTER THREE

FINDING WATER SOURCES: NAVIGATING HYDRATION IN THE WILDERNESS

In wilderness survival for kids, understanding how to find and safely utilize water sources is paramount. This section delves into the importance of staying hydrated, methods for identifying safe water in the wilderness, techniques for purifying water, and the overall significance of responsible hydration practices.

Identifying Safe Water in the Wilderness

Water is an essential component of survival, and teaching kids how to identify safe sources in the wilderness is crucial. While nature offers many water sources, not all are safe for consumption. Instructing children on the following principles ensures they make informed decisions about where to obtain water:

- **Running Water:** Streams, rivers, and creeks often provide safer water than stagnant sources. Running water is less likely to harbor harmful bacteria and contaminants. Teach kids to collect water from these sources, preferably using a clean container.

- **Natural Springs:** Natural springs are another reliable source of clean water. Springs emerge from the ground, often filtered through layers of soil and rocks, making them relatively pure. Emphasize the importance of selecting springs away from human and animal activity.

- **Rainwater:** In certain situations, rainwater can be a viable source. Teach kids how to collect rainwater using improvised containers, such as tarps or large leaves. Ensure they understand the importance of choosing an uncontaminated collection surface.

- **Lakes and Ponds:** While lakes and ponds may seem like convenient water sources, they can harbor harmful microorganisms. Teach kids to prioritize running water or natural springs over stagnant bodies of water. If using water from lakes or ponds, purify it thoroughly.

Techniques for Purifying Water

Even seemingly clean water sources in the wilderness can contain invisible threats, such as bacteria, parasites, and viruses. Teaching kids effective water purification methods ensures they stay healthy and hydrated. The following techniques are suitable for young explorers:

- **Boiling:** Boiling water is one of the most straightforward and effective purification methods. Instruct kids on the importance of bringing water to a rolling boil for at least one minute (or longer at higher altitudes). Emphasize that this method kills most harmful microorganisms.

- **Water Purification Tablets:** Compact and easy to use, water purification tablets are an excellent option for kids. Teach them how to read and follow the instructions on the tablet packaging. Reinforce the importance of waiting the recommended time before consuming the treated water.

- **Portable Water Filters:** Portable water filters provide a convenient and reliable way to purify water. Show kids how to use these devices, including proper setup, filtering techniques, and maintenance. Highlight the importance of selecting a filter suitable for the specific wilderness conditions.

- **Solar Water Disinfection (SODIS):** This method utilizes sunlight to disinfect water. Instruct kids on how to fill a clear container with water and leave it in direct sunlight for at least six hours. Teach them to use containers made of clear PET plastic for optimal results.

- **Improvised Filtration:** In a survival situation, kids can create improvised filters using readily available materials. Show them how to use cloth, sand, and charcoal to filter out debris and impurities. While this method may not eliminate all microorganisms, it can improve water clarity.

The Importance of Hydration

Emphasizing the importance of hydration is foundational in teaching wilderness survival to kids. In the outdoors, maintaining proper hydration levels is critical for overall well-being and the ability to perform essential tasks. Key considerations include:

- **Dehydration Risks:** Teach kids to recognize the signs of dehydration, including thirst, dry mouth, dark urine, fatigue, and dizziness. Explain that dehydration can impede physical and cognitive functions, emphasizing the importance of preventing it.

- **Hydration Guidelines:** Instill the habit of drinking water regularly, even before feeling thirsty. Encourage kids to sip water consistently throughout the day rather than consuming large amounts at once. Discuss the factors influencing hydration needs, such as activity level, weather conditions, and individual health.

- **Water Storage and Management**: Show kids how to manage their water supply responsibly. Discuss strategies for rationing water during extended periods without access to a water source. Reinforce the importance of balancing hydration needs with the availability of water.

- **Environmental Considerations:** Teach kids to be mindful of the environmental impact of their water consumption. Emphasize the Leave No Trace principle of minimizing the impact on water sources, avoiding contamination, and respecting the delicate balance of ecosystems.

- **Rehydration After Activity:** After engaging in physical activities, kids should be aware of the need for rehydration. Teach them to replenish fluids lost through sweat and exertion. Discuss the importance of consuming electrolytes in the form of sports drinks or natural sources like fruits.

- **Monitoring Urine Color:** A simple yet effective way for kids to gauge their hydration status is by monitoring the color of their urine. Encourage them to aim for light yellow or pale straw-colored urine, indicating proper hydration.

- **Water Conservation:** Instill a sense of water conservation in kids by teaching them to use water wisely. This includes minimizing spillage, avoiding unnecessary water wastage, and respecting the principle of taking only what is needed.

By educating kids on identifying safe water sources, purifying water effectively, and understanding the significance of proper hydration, we equip them with essential skills for wilderness survival. These lessons not only contribute to their safety in outdoor environments but also instill a lifelong awareness of responsible water practices, fostering a deeper connection with nature.

CHAPTER FOUR

BUILDING A FIRE: IGNITING ESSENTIAL WILDERNESS SKILLS IN KIDS

learning how to build and manage a fire is a fundamental skill that goes beyond mere warmth. In this section, we explore the importance of fire in the wilderness, fire safety rules for kids, gathering firewood and tinder, different fire-building techniques, and the etiquette associated with cooking and campfires. Instilling these skills not only enhances a child's ability to survive in the wild but also fosters a deeper connection with nature.

Fire Safety Rules for Kids

Before delving into the intricacies of building a fire, it's crucial to instill fire safety rules in kids. Understanding the potential risks and safety measures associated with fire ensures responsible use in the wilderness. Key fire safety rules for kids include:

- **Clearing the Area:** Teach kids to clear a safe area before starting a fire. Remove any dry leaves, twigs, or other flammable materials from the vicinity. Ensure there is ample space between the fire and surrounding vegetation or structures.

- **Supervision:** Emphasize the importance of adult supervision when kids are involved in fire-building activities. An adult should always be present to oversee the process, provide guidance, and ensure safety.

- **Never Leave Unattended:** Instill the rule that a fire should never be left unattended. Before leaving the fire site, ensure it is fully extinguished. Teach kids how to properly extinguish a fire using water and by spreading the embers.

- **Keep a Safe Distance:** Teach kids to maintain a safe distance from the fire. Emphasize the danger of getting too close, and establish a designated area where they can observe and enjoy the fire without risking burns.

- **No Playing with Fire:** Make it clear that fire is a tool, not a toy. Discourage any behavior that involves playing with fire, such as waving sticks or attempting to jump over flames. Reinforce that fire is to be treated with respect and caution.

Fire Extinguishing Knowledge:

- Educate kids on how to extinguish a fire properly. This involves pouring water on the flames, stirring the ashes, and repeating the process until the area is cool to the touch. Ensure they understand the importance of complete extinguishment.

- **Use Appropriate Tools:** When handling fire-building tools, such as lighters or matches, teach kids the importance of using them responsibly. Ensure they understand that these tools are not toys and should only be used under adult supervision.

- **Emergency Protocol:** In the event of an emergency, teach kids the appropriate actions to take. This may include calling for help, evacuating the area, or using a fire extinguisher if available. Reinforce the importance of staying calm and following emergency protocols.

By establishing and reinforcing these fire safety rules, we create a foundation for responsible fire use in the wilderness. These rules not only prioritize safety but also lay the groundwork for developing a lifelong understanding of fire as a valuable tool in outdoor environments.

Gathering Firewood and Tinder

Building a fire in the wilderness requires the ability to gather suitable firewood and tinder. These skills involve understanding the different types of wood, recognizing dry and dead materials, and efficiently collecting resources. Here's a guide to imparting these skills to kids:

Types of Wood

Teach kids to identify the three main types of wood needed for a successful fire:

- **Tinder:** This is the initial material that ignites easily. Examples include dry leaves, grass, or thin bark.

- **Kindling:** These are small sticks or twigs that catch fire from the tinder. They help build the initial flame. Encourage kids to look for small, dry branches.

- **Fuelwood:** This is larger, more substantial wood that sustains the fire once it is established. Fallen branches or logs make suitable fuelwood.

Recognizing Dry and Dead Materials

Emphasize the importance of using dry and dead materials for fire-building. Wet or green wood can be challenging to ignite and will produce more smoke than heat. Teach kids to identify dry, brittle, and dead materials by their appearance and sound.

Responsible Collection

Instruct kids on responsible gathering practices. They should avoid damaging live vegetation and only collect materials that are already dead or fallen. Teach them to use fallen branches and twigs rather than breaking them off living trees.

Efficient Collection Techniques

Show kids how to efficiently collect firewood. Demonstrate proper techniques for gathering tinder, kindling, and fuelwood. This may involve using a knife or a small saw to cut branches into manageable sizes.

Storage and Organization

Teach kids the importance of organizing their firewood before starting a fire. Having tinder, kindling, and fuelwood readily accessible ensures a smooth and efficient fire-building process. Show them how to arrange materials in a pyramid or log cabin structure for optimal burning.

By teaching kids the art of gathering firewood and tinder, we equip them with practical skills that enhance their ability to create and maintain a fire in the wilderness. These skills not only contribute to survival but also deepen their understanding of the natural resources around them.

Different Fire-Building Techniques

Building a fire involves more than just stacking wood and lighting it. Different techniques cater to varying situations and conditions. Introduce kids to diverse fire-building methods to broaden their skill set:

- **Teepee Fire:** The teepee fire is a classic and straightforward method. Start by placing the tinder in the center and arranging kindling sticks around it in a teepee shape. As the fire grows, add larger sticks and fuelwood. This method promotes good airflow, aiding the ignition process.

- **Log Cabin Fire:** In the log cabin method, create a square or rectangular structure using fuelwood, leaving an open space in the center for the tinder and kindling. As the fire burns, the structure collapses inward, providing a steady supply of fuelwood.

- **Lean-To Fire:** Ideal for windy conditions, the lean-to fire involves propping kindling against a larger piece of fuelwood, creating a slope. Place tinder at the base. As the fire ignites, it travels up the slope, catching the fuelwood.

- **Dakota Fire Hole:** The Dakota fire hole is a technique suitable for areas with limited firewood or in windy conditions. Dig a hole in the ground and connect it to a second hole at an angle. Place the tinder and kindling in the first hole and use the second hole as a vent. This method conserves fuelwood and minimizes the visibility of the fire.

- **Upside-Down Fire**: Also known as the top-down fire, this method involves placing the largest fuelwood at the bottom, followed by progressively smaller pieces, with tinder and kindling on top. Igniting the top layer allows the fire to burn downward, providing a longer-lasting flame.

- **Bow Drill Fire:** For a more primitive and hands-on approach, introduce kids to the bow drill method. This involves using a bow, spindle, hearth board, and socket to generate friction and create an ember. While it requires practice and skill, it offers a unique and educational experience.

- **Magnifying Glass or Lens Fire:** Teach kids how to use sunlight and a magnifying glass or lens to start a fire. This method requires focusing sunlight onto tinder to create enough heat for ignition. It's a valuable skill that doesn't rely on matches or lighters.

Cooking and Campfire

- **Etiquette:** While fire is essential for survival, it also plays a significant role in cooking and creating a communal atmosphere in the wilderness. Teaching kids campfire etiquette ensures responsible and enjoyable outdoor experiences. Key considerations include:

- **Responsible Cooking Practices:** Show kids how to use a campfire for cooking. Whether using a portable stove or open flames, emphasize the importance of safe cooking practices, such as keeping a safe distance from the fire and using appropriate cookware.

- **Leave No Trace:** Instill the Leave No Trace principles in kids when it comes to campfires. Teach them to clean up after themselves, pack out all trash, and avoid leaving any trace of their presence. Reinforce the importance of respecting nature and leaving the wilderness as they found it.

- **Fire Size and Duration:** Discuss the appropriate size and duration of a campfire. Emphasize that fires should be small and manageable, and they should be extinguished completely before leaving the area. Teach kids to use the minimum amount of fuelwood necessary for cooking or warmth.

- **Respecting Wildlife:** Highlight the importance of respecting wildlife when building and maintaining a campfire. Fires can disrupt local fauna, so teach kids to choose a location away from animal habitats. Reinforce the need to observe wildlife from a distance without disturbing their natural behavior.

- **Fire Circle Etiquette:** When camping with others, teach kids about fire circle etiquette. Emphasize the importance of maintaining a safe distance between individuals and the fire. Instruct them on how to situate themselves around the fire without crowding or creating safety hazards.

- **Extinguishing the Fire:** Teach kids the proper procedure for extinguishing a campfire. This involves pouring water on the flames, stirring the embers, and repeating the process until the fire site is cool to the touch. Reinforce the importance of leaving no smoldering embers behind.

By incorporating these fire-building techniques and campfire etiquette into their wilderness survival skill set, kids not only enhance their ability to thrive in outdoor environments but also develop a profound appreciation for the role of fire in nature. These skills contribute to responsible and sustainable outdoor practices, fostering a connection with the wilderness that goes beyond survival.

CHAPTER FIVE

CONSTRUCTING A SHELTER: CRAFTING WILDERNESS REFUGES FOR KIDS

In the world of wilderness survival for kids, the ability to construct a shelter is a vital skill that ensures protection from the elements and promotes a sense of security in the great outdoors. This section explores the basics of shelter construction, understanding shelter principles, emergency shelter building, and utilizing natural resources to create a safe haven. By imparting these skills to children, we equip them with the knowledge to thrive in different environments and scenarios.

Understanding Shelter Basics

Before delving into the practical aspects of shelter construction, it's essential for kids to understand the basic principles that govern the creation of effective shelters. The primary goals of a wilderness shelter are to provide protection from the elements, maintain body temperature, and ensure a safe and secure space for rest. Key principles include:

1. **Location:** Choose a shelter location that is elevated, dry, and away from potential hazards such as flash floods or falling branches. Take advantage of natural features like hills or rock formations for added protection.

2. **Insulation:** The shelter should provide insulation against extreme temperatures. This can be achieved by using natural materials such as leaves, grass, or even snow, depending on the environment.

3. **Ventilation:** Proper ventilation prevents condensation inside the shelter, reducing the risk of hypothermia. Leave openings for fresh air circulation while maintaining a balance to block wind and rain.

4. **Size and Proportion:** The shelter should be appropriately sized for the number of occupants to maximize body heat retention. It should also be proportionate to the surrounding environment to minimize visual impact.

5. **Materials:** Utilize available materials in the environment, such as branches, leaves, or snow, to construct the shelter. This not only ensures compatibility with the surroundings but also conserves energy and resources.

6. **Accessibility:** Ensure the shelter is easily accessible and does not require excessive energy or time to construct. In

emergency situations, a quick and simple shelter can be more crucial than an elaborate one.

Emergency Shelter Building

Teaching kids how to build an emergency shelter is a valuable skill that can make a significant difference in unexpected situations. Whether lost in the wilderness or caught in adverse weather conditions, the ability to create a makeshift shelter quickly can be a lifesaver. The following steps outline a simple emergency shelter-building process for kids:

Step 1: Assess the Environment

Encourage kids to assess their surroundings before building a shelter. Look for natural features like large rocks, fallen trees, or overhangs that can provide additional protection. Consider the direction of the wind and the potential for weather changes.

Step 2: Gather Materials

Show kids how to gather materials for the shelter. Depending on the environment, this may include branches, leaves, grass, or even snow. Emphasize the importance of choosing dry materials to enhance insulation.

Step 3: Choose a Shelter Design

Introduce kids to basic shelter designs that are easy to construct in emergency situations. A simple lean-to or A-frame shelter is often effective. These designs require minimal materials and can be adapted to various environments.

Step 4: Construct the Frame

Demonstrate how to construct the frame of the shelter using sturdy branches or saplings. The frame should be securely anchored to the ground and provide a stable structure for the shelter.

Step 5: Add Insulating Materials

Once the frame is in place, show kids how to layer insulating materials over it. This may include leaves, grass, or even additional branches to create a barrier against wind and cold temperatures.

Step 6: Cover the Shelter

Cover the frame with additional materials to create a protective layer. For example, if using a lean-to design, place large leaves or branches at an angle against the frame to block wind and rain.

Step 7: Create a Sleeping Area

Inside the shelter, clear a space for a sleeping area. This can be achieved by flattening the ground and adding a layer of insulating materials. Teach kids to arrange the materials in a way that provides a comfortable and dry surface.

Step 8: Seal Gaps

Ensure that gaps in the shelter are sealed to minimize drafts. Use additional materials to cover any openings or spaces between branches. This helps retain body heat inside the shelter.

Step 9: Test the Shelter

Encourage kids to enter the shelter and assess its effectiveness. This hands-on experience allows them to understand the importance of proper construction and insulation.

Step 10: Make Adjustments

Based on the test, make any necessary adjustments to improve the shelter's functionality. This may involve adding more insulation, adjusting the angle of branches, or reinforcing the frame for stability.

By practicing emergency shelter-building, kids not only gain valuable survival skills but also develop problem-solving abilities and resourcefulness. These skills instill a sense of empowerment, fostering confidence in their ability to navigate unforeseen challenges in the wilderness.

Utilizing Natural Resources for Shelter

Teaching kids to utilize natural resources for shelter construction not only enhances their survival skills but also instills a deep appreciation for the environment. Here are ways to incorporate natural resources into shelter-building activities:

1. **Branches and Saplings:** Demonstrate how to identify and select suitable branches or saplings for constructing the frame of the shelter. Emphasize the importance of choosing materials that are sturdy and free from signs of decay.

2. **Leaves and Grass:** Show kids how to gather leaves and grass to create insulation layers for the shelter. Discuss the properties of different types of leaves and grass, highlighting their insulating and moisture-resistant qualities.

3. **Rocks and Stones:** In rocky environments, teach kids how to use rocks and stones strategically. These can be arranged

to create windbreaks, anchor the shelter frame, or elevate the sleeping area to avoid cold ground contact.

4. Snow: In snowy conditions, demonstrate the technique of building a snow shelter, such as a quinzhee or snow cave. Teach kids to compact snow for building blocks and create an insulated space inside the structure.

5. Bark and Tree Debris: Discuss the use of bark and tree debris for shelter construction. Certain types of bark can be flexible and used for weaving or tying components of the shelter together. Tree debris, such as small twigs, can add additional insulation.

6. Moss and Lichens: In certain environments, moss and lichens can be used for additional insulation or as a covering material. Teach kids to recognize different types of moss and lichens and their suitability for shelter construction.

7. Vines and Cordage: Introduce the concept of using natural vines or cordage made from plant fibers for securing components of the shelter. Demonstrate basic knot-tying techniques that can be useful in shelter construction.

8. Animal Materials: Discuss the ethical considerations of using materials from animals, such as feathers or fur, for insulation. Emphasize the importance of respecting wildlife and utilizing only materials that are naturally shed or obtained without harm.

By incorporating natural resources into shelter-building activities, kids not only enhance their survival skills but also develop a deeper understanding of the interconnectedness of nature. This approach fosters a sense of responsibility for the environment and encourages sustainable practices in outdoor activities.

Conclusion

The ability to construct a shelter is a foundational skill in the realm of wilderness survival for kids. By understanding shelter principles, practicing emergency shelter-building, and utilizing natural resources, children not only enhance their ability to thrive in the great outdoors but also develop problem-solving skills, resourcefulness, and a profound connection with nature. These skills contribute to a sense of self-reliance and empowerment, ensuring that young adventurers are well-equipped to navigate diverse environments and scenarios in the wilderness.

CHAPTER SIX

NAVIGATION IN THE WILDERNESS: NAVIGATING THE WILD WITH CONFIDENCE

In the expansive realm of wilderness survival for kids, the ability to navigate effectively is a skill that goes beyond reading maps and using a compass. This section explores the importance of navigation, essential tools for wilderness navigation, basic map-reading skills, orienteering techniques, and strategies for staying on course. By instilling these navigation skills in children, we empower them to explore the outdoors with confidence, fostering a sense of adventure and self-sufficiency.

Understanding the Importance of Navigation

Navigation is a fundamental skill that plays a pivotal role in wilderness survival for kids. Whether exploring hiking trails, camping in remote areas, or participating in outdoor activities, the ability to navigate effectively ensures safety, prevents getting lost, and enhances the overall outdoor experience. Here are key aspects that underscore the importance of navigation for kids:

1. Safety: Navigation skills contribute to safety by helping kids stay on designated trails, avoid hazardous areas, and reach their destination without unnecessary risks. This is particularly crucial in unfamiliar terrain.

2. Confidence: Proficiency in navigation builds confidence. Kids who can read maps, use a compass, and follow trail markers feel more self-assured in their outdoor adventures. This confidence extends to decision-making and problem-solving in unfamiliar environments.

3. Preventing Getting Lost: Knowing how to navigate prevents the anxiety and potential dangers associated with getting lost in the wilderness. Kids equipped with navigation skills can confidently explore, knowing they have the tools to find their way back.

4. Environmental Awareness: Navigation fosters environmental awareness by encouraging kids to observe and interpret natural features, landmarks, and signs. This heightened awareness enhances their connection with nature and the ability to appreciate the beauty of the outdoors.

5. Independence: Navigation skills promote independence. Kids who can navigate effectively are less reliant on constant guidance, allowing them to explore and enjoy the wilderness with a greater sense of autonomy.

6. Planning and Preparedness: Navigation involves planning routes, understanding topography, and being prepared for the journey. This planning aspect instills a mindset of preparedness, ensuring that kids have the necessary resources and knowledge for their outdoor adventures.

Essential Tools for Wilderness Navigation

To navigate the wilderness successfully, kids need to be familiar with and proficient in using essential navigation tools. These tools provide the foundation for effective orientation and route planning. The key tools for wilderness navigation include:

1. Map:

- Teach kids how to read and interpret topographic maps. Explain contour lines, symbols, and scale.

- Emphasize the importance of choosing the right map for the specific area they are exploring.

- Familiarize them with map legends to understand the symbols and markings used on the map.

2. Compass:

- Instruct kids on how to use a compass for orientation. Teach them about cardinal directions (north, south, east, west) and how to align the compass with the map.

- Show them how to adjust for magnetic declination to ensure accurate navigation.

- Demonstrate basic compass navigation techniques, such as taking bearings and following a bearing.

3. GPS Device:

- Introduce kids to the basics of using a GPS device for navigation. Teach them how to read coordinates, set waypoints, and navigate to a destination.

- Emphasize the importance of using a GPS device as a supplementary tool rather than a sole reliance on technology.

4. Trail Markers:

- Educate kids about common trail markers used in hiking and outdoor activities. These may include colored blazes, cairns, or signage.

- Emphasize the significance of staying on marked trails for safety and environmental conservation.

5. Observational Skills:

- Instill the habit of observation. Teach kids to identify natural features, landmarks, and distinctive terrain characteristics.

- Show them how to use these observations for navigation, such as recognizing a prominent mountain or distinctive tree as a reference point.

Basic Map-Reading Skills

To navigate effectively, kids must develop basic map-reading skills. This involves understanding the information presented on a topographic map and translating it into actionable navigation decisions. Here are key map-reading skills to teach kids:

1. Understanding Contour Lines:

- Explain the concept of contour lines and their representation of elevation on the map.

- Teach kids how to identify hills, valleys, and flat areas by interpreting the spacing and shape of contour lines.

2. Map Scale:

- Familiarize kids with the map scale. Help them understand the relationship between distances on the map and actual distances in the wilderness.

- Show them how to use the scale to estimate travel times and distances.

3. Map Orientation:

- Emphasize the importance of aligning the map with the terrain. Teach kids how to use a compass to orient the map to the cardinal directions.

- Show them how to match landmarks on the map with features in the environment to confirm orientation.

4. Identifying Symbols and Legends:

- Introduce kids to map legends and symbols. Teach them to interpret symbols representing trails, water bodies, roads, and other features.

- Demonstrate how to use the legend to understand the meaning of different markings on the map.

5. Locating Coordinates:

- If using a GPS device or working with specific coordinates, teach kids how to locate and read latitude and longitude on the map.

- Show them how to plot coordinates and navigate to a specific location using the map.

Orienteering Techniques for Kids

Orienteering is a valuable activity that combines navigation skills with physical exercise. It's an excellent way to reinforce navigation concepts while engaging kids in an interactive and enjoyable experience. Here are orienteering techniques suitable for kids:

1. Map and Compass Courses:

- Set up simple map and compass courses in a safe outdoor area. Include checkpoints marked on the map, and challenge kids to navigate from point to point using their compass and map-reading skills.

2. Scavenger Hunts:

- Organize orienteering scavenger hunts where kids follow a map to find hidden items or markers. This activity combines navigation with problem-solving and teamwork.

3. Nature Bingo:

- Create nature bingo cards featuring different natural features or landmarks. Kids can use their maps to navigate and mark off items as they find them.

4. Geocaching:

- Introduce geocaching, a modern form of treasure hunting using GPS coordinates. Hide small containers with logbooks and treasures in the wilderness, and encourage kids to find them using GPS devices.

5. Relay Races:

- Organize relay races where teams must navigate a course, passing a baton or designated item between team members. This adds an element of competition and teamwork to the orienteering experience.

Strategies for Staying on Course

Navigating the wilderness is not just about knowing where to go but also about staying on course throughout the journey. Teach kids strategies for maintaining their direction and preventing deviations:

1. Regular Map Checks:

- Emphasize the importance of regularly checking the map to ensure alignment with the terrain. Encourage kids to establish a routine of map checks at key waypoints or intervals.

2. Landmark Identification:

- Teach kids to identify and memorize prominent landmarks along their route. Using recognizable features helps them stay oriented and confirm their location.

3. Following Trail Markers:

- If on a marked trail, instruct kids to follow trail markers consistently. Reinforce the idea that straying off the trail can lead to confusion and difficulty in finding the way back.

4. Backtracking:

- If uncertain about the route, teach kids the strategy of backtracking. Returning to a known point and reassessing the map can help identify any mistakes or deviations.

5. Maintaining a Bearing:

- For off-trail navigation, show kids how to maintain a compass bearing. Emphasize the importance of periodically checking the compass to stay on the intended course.

6. Using Natural Features:

- Encourage kids to use natural features as navigation aids. This may include following a river, ridge, or other distinctive terrain features to stay on course.

7. Creating Mental Landmarks:

- Help kids develop the skill of creating mental landmarks. This involves noting unique features in the environment and associating them with specific points on the map.

8. Team Communication:

- If navigating as a group, stress the importance of effective communication. Encourage kids to share observations, confirm directions, and collectively make navigation decisions.

By imparting navigation skills to kids, we equip them with the tools and knowledge needed to explore the wilderness confidently and responsibly. These skills contribute to a sense of adventure, independence, and environmental awareness, laying the foundation for a lifelong appreciation of outdoor exploration. The ability to navigate the wild with confidence not only enhances safety but also fosters a deeper connection with the natural world.

CHAPTER SEVEN

IDENTIFYING EDIBLE PLANTS AND WILDLIFE: NOURISHMENT FROM NATURE IN WILDERNESS SURVIVAL FOR KIDS

The ability to identify edible plants and wildlife is a skill that not only enhances their connection with nature but also ensures a sustainable source of nourishment in the great outdoors. This section explores the importance of foraging, key principles of plant and wildlife identification, common edible plants, ethical foraging practices, and safety considerations. By instilling these skills in children, we empower them to responsibly explore and sustain themselves in diverse wilderness environments.

The Importance of Foraging in Wilderness Survival

Foraging, or the act of searching for food in the wild, is a fundamental skill that has been crucial for human survival throughout history. In the context of wilderness survival for kids, foraging serves several important purposes:

1. **Nourishment:** Identifying edible plants and wildlife provides a sustainable source of nourishment in the absence

of traditional food sources. This is especially valuable in survival situations or during outdoor adventures.

2. Connection with Nature: Foraging fosters a deeper connection with the natural world. It encourages kids to observe and appreciate the diversity of plant and animal life, promoting environmental awareness and respect for ecosystems.

3. Self-Sufficiency: Learning to identify and harvest edible plants and wildlife instills a sense of self-sufficiency. Kids gain confidence in their ability to find food in the wild, enhancing their overall wilderness survival skills.

4. Culinary Exploration: Foraging opens the door to culinary exploration. Kids can learn about the flavors, textures, and nutritional benefits of different wild foods, expanding their palate and culinary knowledge.

5. Survival Skills: In emergency situations, the ability to forage for food becomes a critical survival skill. Understanding which plants are safe to eat and how to responsibly harvest wildlife can make a significant difference in a survival scenario.

Principles of Plant and Wildlife Identification

Before delving into specific edible plants and wildlife, it's essential to instill foundational principles of identification in kids. This involves teaching them to observe, recognize key characteristics, and make informed decisions about the edibility of plants and animals. Key principles include:

1. Observation Skills:

 - Encourage kids to develop keen observation skills. This involves paying attention to details such as leaf shape, color, size, and growth patterns for plants, and fur, feathers, size, and behavior for wildlife.

2. Field Guides and Resources:

 - Introduce the use of field guides and reliable resources for plant and wildlife identification. Teach kids how to use these references to cross-reference their observations and make accurate identifications.

3. Distinctive Features:

 - Emphasize the importance of identifying distinctive features. For plants, this may include unique leaves, flowers, or fruit. For wildlife, it could be specific markings, tracks, or behaviors.

4. Toxicity Awareness:

- Instill an understanding of the potential dangers of toxic plants and wildlife. Teach kids to prioritize safety and avoid consuming anything they are uncertain about.

5. Seasonal Variations:

- Highlight the importance of considering seasonal variations. Some plants may be edible in certain seasons but toxic in others. Wildlife behavior and availability can also change with the seasons.

6. Habitat Considerations:

- Discuss the relevance of habitat when identifying plants and wildlife. Certain species thrive in specific environments, and recognizing these habitats aids in accurate identification.

7. Local Knowledge:

- Foster an appreciation for local knowledge and indigenous wisdom. Understanding the plants and wildlife indigenous to a specific region enhances accurate identification and ensures responsible foraging practices.

Common Edible Plants

Teaching kids to identify common edible plants in the wilderness broadens their foraging capabilities and enriches their understanding of the natural world. While the edibility of plants can vary by region, here are some examples of widely recognized edible plants:

1. Dandelion (Taraxacum officinale):

- Identification: Recognized by its distinctive yellow flowers and toothed leaves. All parts of the plant are edible, including leaves, flowers, and roots.

- Edible Parts: Young leaves can be added to salads, while flowers can be used for tea or as a garnish. The roots can be roasted and used as a coffee substitute.

2. Wild Strawberries (Fragaria vesca):

- **Identification:** Small, red berries with distinctive seeds on the surface. Leaves are compound with three leaflets.

- **Edible Parts:** The sweet berries are edible and can be eaten fresh or used in jams and desserts. The leaves can be used for making tea.

3. Plantain (Plantago major):

- **Identification:** Broad, ribbed leaves with a rosette pattern. Commonly found in lawns and disturbed areas.

- **Edible Parts:** Young leaves are edible and can be added to salads or cooked as greens. Plantain has medicinal properties and can be used for soothing skin irritations.

4. Burdock (Arctium lappa):

- **Identification:** Large, heart-shaped leaves and prickly burrs that cling to clothing or animal fur.

- **Edible Parts:** The root of the burdock plant is edible and can be cooked or used in soups. Young leaves can also be consumed after boiling.

5. Chickweed (Stellaria media):

- **Identification:** Small, star-like white flowers and opposite pairs of lance-shaped leaves.

- **Edible Parts:** Chickweed leaves and stems are edible and can be added to salads or used in sandwiches. It has a mild, fresh flavor.

6. Pine (Pinus spp.) Nuts:

- **Identification:** Pine trees are easily recognizable by their needle-like leaves and cones.

- **Edible Parts:** Pine nuts, found inside the cones, are edible and nutritious. They can be eaten raw or roasted and used in various dishes.

7. Stinging Nettle (Urtica dioica):

- **Identification:** Toothed, opposite leaves with tiny hairs that can cause skin irritation.

- **Edible Parts:** Young, tender nettle leaves are edible when cooked and can be used in soups, stews, or as a substitute for spinach.

8. Blackberries (Rubus fruticosus):

- **Identification:** Clusters of dark purple to black berries on thorny canes.

- **Edible Parts:** The sweet berries are edible and can be eaten fresh, used in desserts, or made into jams and preserves.

Ethical Foraging Practices

Responsible foraging is essential for maintaining ecological balance and preserving natural habitats. Instilling ethical foraging practices in kids ensures they approach wild food sources with respect and sustainability. Here are key principles of ethical foraging:

1. Leave No Trace:

- Teach kids the Leave No Trace principles, emphasizing the importance of minimizing their impact on the environment. This includes avoiding damage to plants and habitats.

2. Harvest Responsibly:

- Instruct kids to harvest plants in a responsible manner. Only take what is needed, and avoid depleting entire populations. Harvesting leaves or fruits while leaving the root or main plant intact promotes regrowth.

3. Avoid Rare or Endangered Species:

- Emphasize the importance of avoiding foraging for rare or endangered plant species. Focus on abundant and common species that can withstand harvesting pressure.

4. Respect Wildlife:

- Teach kids to respect wildlife and their habitats. Avoid disturbing nests, dens, or feeding areas. Responsible foraging considers the broader ecosystem and its inhabitants.

5. Know Local Regulations:

- Instill the habit of knowing and adhering to local regulations regarding foraging. Some areas may have restrictions on collecting certain plants or interacting with wildlife.

6. Learn Proper Identification:

- Stress the significance of accurate plant and wildlife identification. Misidentification can lead to unintentional harm to ecosystems or health risks.

7. Cultivate Awareness of Invasive Species:

- Educate kids about invasive plant species and their impact on native ecosystems. Discourage foraging for invasive species, as it may contribute to their spread.

8. Seasonal Considerations:

- Highlight the importance of considering the seasonality of wild foods. Some plants may be protected during specific seasons to allow for reproduction and growth.

Safety Considerations in Foraging

While foraging for edible plants and wildlife can be a rewarding experience, it is essential to prioritize safety. Teach kids to approach foraging with caution and to follow these safety considerations:

1. Be 100% Certain of Identification:

- Stress the importance of being absolutely certain about the identification of plants and wildlife before consumption. Misidentification can lead to poisoning or adverse reactions.

2. Avoid Toxic Look-Alikes:

- Teach kids to be aware of toxic look-alikes. Some edible plants have poisonous counterparts that closely resemble them. Ensure they can differentiate between the two.

3. Know Allergies and Sensitivities:

- Instruct kids to be aware of any allergies or sensitivities they may have to specific plants or wildlife. Avoid foraging for items that may trigger adverse reactions.

4. Avoid Polluted Areas:

- Discourage foraging in areas with potential pollution, such as industrial sites, roadsides, or areas sprayed with pesticides. Wild foods from contaminated environments can pose health risks.

5. Wash and Cook Wild Foods:

- Emphasize the importance of washing wild foods thoroughly to remove any contaminants. Cooking wild foods also reduces the risk of pathogens.

6. Be Mindful of Conservation Areas:

- In conservation areas or protected ecosystems, discourage foraging to avoid disrupting fragile habitats or endangering rare species.

7. Respect Private Property:

- Teach kids to respect private property rights. Foraging on private land without permission is not only unethical but may also pose safety risks.

8. Stay Hydrated:

- Remind kids to stay hydrated, especially during foraging activities. Carry water and be mindful of the importance of maintaining proper hydration in the wilderness.

By combining the excitement of foraging with a commitment to safety, ethical practices, and ecological awareness, kids can develop a well-rounded understanding of their role in the natural world. The ability to identify edible plants and wildlife not only contributes to survival skills but also nurtures a profound connection with nature. This connection fosters a sense of responsibility for the environment and a lifelong appreciation for the diverse offerings of the wild.

CHAPTER EIGHT

SURVIVAL GAMES AND DRILLS FOR KIDS: FOSTERING SKILLS, CONFIDENCE, AND FUN IN THE WILDERNESS

Engaging kids in survival games and drills not only introduces them to valuable wilderness skills but also turns learning into an enjoyable and interactive experience. This section explores the importance of survival games for kids, key skills addressed through games and drills, and provides examples of entertaining and educational activities that instill a sense of adventure, confidence, and preparedness in young adventurers.

Importance of Survival Games for Kids

Survival games for kids serve as an effective and enjoyable means of imparting essential wilderness skills. These games go beyond traditional teaching methods, transforming learning into a dynamic and interactive process. Here's why survival games are beneficial for kids:

1. Hands-On Learning:

- Survival games immerse kids in hands-on learning experiences. Instead of simply hearing about survival techniques, they actively participate, reinforcing practical skills.

2. Problem-Solving Skills:

- Many survival games involve problem-solving scenarios. Kids learn to think critically, make decisions, and adapt to changing situations—an invaluable skill set in the wilderness.

3. Teamwork and Communication:

- Cooperative survival games foster teamwork and communication. Kids collaborate to overcome challenges, enhancing their ability to work together in real-life outdoor situations.

4. Boosting Confidence:

- Successfully navigating survival challenges in a controlled and playful setting builds confidence. Kids develop a sense of accomplishment, knowing they can handle various scenarios.

5. Making Learning Fun:

- Survival games transform learning into an entertaining adventure. Kids are more likely to retain information when it's presented in a fun and engaging manner.

6. Preparedness Mindset:

- Survival games instill a preparedness mindset. By simulating potential survival situations, kids become more mentally and emotionally equipped to handle emergencies.

Key Skills Addressed Through Survival Games and Drills

Survival games and drills for kids cover a range of essential skills that are valuable in outdoor environments. These activities address core aspects of wilderness survival and foster a holistic approach to preparedness. Here are key skills commonly addressed through survival games:

1. Navigation:

- Orienteering games involve using maps and compasses to navigate through a course. This builds kids' ability to read maps, follow directions, and stay oriented in the wilderness.

2. Fire Building:

- Fire-building games teach kids to create fire using various methods. This includes using fire starters, friction-based methods, or even magnifying glasses. Learning to build a fire is a fundamental survival skill.

3. Shelter Construction:

- Shelter-building games challenge kids to construct makeshift shelters using natural materials. This enhances their understanding of shelter principles and the importance of protection from the elements.

4. First Aid Skills:

- First aid games simulate injuries or medical emergencies. Kids learn basic first aid skills such as wound care, CPR, and handling common outdoor injuries.

5. Foraging and Plant Identification:

- Foraging games introduce kids to edible plants and wildlife. They learn to identify safe-to-eat plants, understand ethical foraging practices, and gain knowledge about local flora.

6. Water Sourcing and Purification:

- Water-related games focus on finding and purifying water. Kids explore methods like natural filtration, boiling, or using purification tablets to make water safe for consumption.

7. Survival Scenarios:

- Scenario-based games present simulated survival situations. Kids must apply their knowledge to make decisions, prioritize needs, and overcome challenges in a controlled environment.

8. Knot-Tying Skills:

- Knot-tying games teach kids various knots used in outdoor activities. From securing shelters to creating makeshift tools, knot-tying is a versatile skill in survival scenarios.

9. Campfire Cooking:

- Cooking games involve preparing meals over a campfire. Kids learn about safe cooking practices, utilizing available resources, and preparing simple, nourishing meals in the wilderness.

10. Emergency Signaling:

- Signaling games focus on emergency communication. Kids use signals like whistles, mirrors, or improvised signs to convey messages and understand the importance of communication in survival situations.

Survival Games and Drills: Examples and Descriptions

1. Orienteering Adventure:

- Set up an orienteering course with checkpoints marked on a map. Kids use compasses to navigate from point to point, enhancing their map-reading and compass skills. This game can be adapted to different terrains and difficulty levels.

2. Survivor Shelter Challenge:

- Challenge kids to construct shelters using available materials. Provide basic guidelines on shelter principles and let them use creativity to build structures. This fosters teamwork, creativity, and an understanding of shelter essentials.

3. Fire-Building Relay:

- Organize a relay race where teams compete to build a fire. Each team member contributes to a specific step, such as gathering tinder, building the structure, or lighting the fire. This game reinforces fire-building skills and teamwork.

4. Wilderness First Aid Simulation:

- Create scenarios simulating outdoor injuries or medical emergencies. Equip kids with basic first aid supplies and guide them through the process of assessing, treating, and responding to different situations. This game enhances their first aid skills and decision-making abilities.

5. Foraging Scavenger Hunt:

- Organize a scavenger hunt where kids search for edible plants or items representing them. Provide information on local flora and ethical foraging practices. This game combines learning about edible plants with the excitement of a scavenger hunt.

6. Water Sourcing Relay:

- Set up a relay race focused on water sourcing. Kids use different methods to collect water, such as creating improvised filters or using natural sources. This game reinforces the importance of water in survival scenarios.

7. Survival Trivia Challenge:

- Develop a trivia challenge covering various survival skills. Create questions related to navigation, shelter construction, plant identification, and other key topics. Kids can compete individually or in teams, reinforcing their knowledge in a fun format.

8. Knot-Tying Olympics:

- Turn knot-tying into a fun and competitive activity. Set up stations with different knots and challenge kids to tie them accurately within a specified time. This game enhances their knot-tying skills in an engaging way.

9. Campfire Cooking Cook-Off:

- Organize a cook-off where kids prepare meals over a campfire. Provide a variety of ingredients, and let them use their creativity to cook nourishing meals. This game combines outdoor cooking skills with an element of friendly competition.

10. Emergency Signaling Relay:

- Create a relay race focusing on emergency signaling. Kids practice using whistles, mirrors, or other signaling tools to convey messages over a distance. This game reinforces the importance of communication in survival situations.

Tips for Organizing and Facilitating Survival Games for Kids

1. Safety First:

- Prioritize safety in all activities. Ensure that games are age-appropriate, and provide proper supervision. Emphasize safety guidelines for handling tools, fire, and outdoor activities.

2. Adapt to Ages and Abilities:

- Tailor games to the ages and abilities of the participants. Adjust the complexity of challenges based on the group's experience and familiarity with outdoor activities.

3. Incorporate Learning Moments:

 - Use downtime between games for brief learning moments. Share interesting facts about plants, wildlife, or survival techniques. This enhances the educational aspect of the activities.

4. Encourage Teamwork:

  - Foster a sense of teamwork and collaboration. Many survival scenarios involve working together, and these games provide opportunities for kids to develop effective communication and cooperation skills.

5. Celebrate Achievements:

  - Celebrate the achievements of participants. Acknowledge their efforts, problem-solving skills, and creativity. Positive reinforcement enhances the overall experience and encourages continued interest in survival skills.

6. Rotate Roles:

  - Allow participants to rotate through different roles in activities. For example, in a shelter-building game, one child may focus on gathering materials, while another takes the lead in construction. This ensures everyone gets a chance to practice various skills.

7. Create a Sense of Adventure:

- Infuse a sense of adventure into the games. Use storytelling elements, create a themed setting, or introduce challenges that spark the imagination. The goal is to make the experience both educational and exciting.

8. Provide Constructive Feedback:

- Offer constructive feedback during and after games. Highlight areas where participants excelled and provide gentle guidance on areas for improvement. This fosters a positive learning environment.

9. Promote Environmental Stewardship:

- Emphasize the importance of respecting the environment. Encourage kids to leave no trace, avoid unnecessary damage to plants or wildlife, and appreciate the beauty of the natural world.

10. Adapt to the Setting:

- Adapt games to the specific setting. Whether in a forest, park, or backyard, tailor activities to the available resources and terrain. This flexibility ensures that games are accessible and enjoyable in diverse environments.

Conclusion

Survival games and drills for kids go beyond imparting practical skills—they foster a love for adventure, a sense of confidence, and a mindset of preparedness. These activities turn learning into a dynamic and enjoyable experience, creating a foundation for a lifelong appreciation of the outdoors. As kids engage in orienteering adventures, fire-building relays, and foraging scavenger hunts, they not only acquire valuable survival skills but also develop a deep connection with nature and a sense of self-sufficiency. The memories of these adventures become stepping stones in their journey of exploration, resilience, and a lifelong passion for the great outdoors.

CHAPTER NINE

EMERGENCY SITUATIONS AND CALLING FOR HELP: EMPOWERING KIDS WITH LIFESAVING SKILLS

In the realm of wilderness survival for kids, understanding how to navigate emergency situations and call for help is a crucial skill. This section explores the importance of preparing children for emergencies, key principles of emergency response, practical steps for calling for help, and ways to instill a sense of responsibility and confidence in young adventurers.

Importance of Emergency Preparedness for Kids

While the great outdoors offers endless opportunities for exploration and adventure, it also presents potential risks and challenges. Teaching kids about emergency situations and the appropriate response is essential for several reasons:

1. Safety First:

 - The primary goal of emergency preparedness is the safety of children. Equipping them with the knowledge and skills to respond effectively in emergencies reduces risks and promotes their well-being in outdoor environments.

2. Empowerment and Confidence:

- Knowing how to handle emergency situations empowers kids and boosts their confidence. When children understand the steps to take in various scenarios, they are more likely to stay calm and make informed decisions.

3. Fostering Responsibility:

- Emergency preparedness instills a sense of responsibility in kids. They learn to prioritize safety, communicate effectively, and take appropriate actions to protect themselves and others.

4. Community and Teamwork:

- Preparedness extends beyond individual actions—it promotes a sense of community and teamwork. Kids learn that in emergency situations, working together and supporting one another is crucial for a positive outcome.

5. Life-Long Skills:

- The skills acquired through emergency preparedness are valuable throughout life. Whether in outdoor adventures, daily activities, or unexpected situations, the ability to assess, respond, and seek help is a lifelong skillset.

Key Principles of Emergency Response for Kids

Teaching kids the fundamentals of emergency response involves instilling key principles that guide their actions in various situations. These principles create a foundation for effective decision-making and communication. Here are key principles of emergency response for kids:

1. Stay Calm:

- Emphasize the importance of staying calm in emergency situations. Fear and panic can hinder effective decision-making. Teach kids relaxation techniques and the value of taking a moment to assess the situation.

2. Assess the Situation:

- Train kids to assess their surroundings and the nature of the emergency. Understanding the context allows them to prioritize actions and make informed decisions about the next steps.

3. Ensure Personal Safety:

- Prioritize personal safety. Teach kids to assess potential dangers and take measures to protect themselves from immediate threats. This may involve moving to a safe location or finding shelter.

4. Call for Help:

- Instill the importance of calling for help in emergency situations. Teach kids how to use communication devices, such as phones or radios, and when and how to contact emergency services or trusted adults.

5. Follow First Aid Basics:

- Introduce basic first aid principles. Kids should know how to address common injuries, perform CPR if necessary, and provide assistance to others in need. First aid skills can make a significant difference in emergencies.

6. Communicate Clearly:

- Effective communication is vital. Teach kids to articulate their location, the nature of the emergency, and any injuries or concerns clearly and concisely. This facilitates a quicker and more accurate response from authorities or caregivers.

7. Stay Together (If in a Group):

- In group settings, stress the importance of staying together. Children should know the designated meeting points or rally locations in case of separation. This principle fosters a sense of accountability and ensures everyone's safety.

8. Use Available Resources:

- Encourage resourcefulness by using available tools and resources. This may include creating signals, using basic survival tools, or improvising solutions to address immediate needs.

Practical Steps for Calling for Help

Teaching kids how to call for help is a practical and crucial aspect of emergency preparedness. The ability to communicate effectively in various scenarios empowers children to seek assistance when needed. Here are practical steps for calling for help:

1. Know Emergency Numbers:

- Ensure that kids know the emergency contact numbers for their region. Teach them to dial these numbers on a phone and explain when it is appropriate to call for emergency services.

2. Identify Trusted Adults:

- In addition to emergency services, identify trusted adults whom kids can contact in case of need. This may include parents, guardians, teachers, or neighbors. Teach kids the importance of having a list of trusted contacts readily available.

3. Use Communication Devices:

- Familiarize kids with communication devices they may encounter, such as phones, radios, or walkie-talkies. Teach them how to unlock and use phones, access contacts, and communicate effectively in different situations.

4. Provide Clear Information:

- Emphasize the importance of providing clear and accurate information. Teach kids to state their name, location, the nature of the emergency, and any relevant details. Clarity in communication facilitates a more effective response.

5. Practice Emergency Calls:

- Conduct practice sessions for making emergency calls. Simulate scenarios where kids must call for help and guide them through the process. Rehearsing these actions helps build confidence and familiarity.

6. Understand Phone Features:

- Teach kids about specific features on phones, such as the location-sharing function. This can be valuable in situations where they are unable to provide their exact location verbally.

7. Use Visual Signals:

- In outdoor settings, teach kids to use visual signals to attract attention. This may include waving brightly colored objects, creating signals with rocks or sticks, or using reflective materials to catch the attention of rescuers.

8. Seek Help from Passersby:

   - In public spaces, kids should know how to approach and seek help from passersby. Teach them to identify safe individuals, such as law enforcement officers or store personnel, and ask for assistance.

Instilling a Sense of Responsibility and Confidence

Beyond teaching specific emergency response skills, fostering a sense of responsibility and confidence in kids contributes to their overall preparedness. Here are ways to instill these qualities:

1. Encourage Problem-Solving:

   - Foster problem-solving skills by presenting scenarios and encouraging kids to think through potential solutions. This helps them develop a proactive mindset in emergency situations.

2. Discuss Real-Life Examples:

- Share age-appropriate real-life examples of emergency situations and their outcomes. Discuss what went well and what could have been done differently. These discussions enhance awareness and preparedness.

3. Set Clear Expectations:

- Clearly communicate expectations regarding responsible behavior in outdoor environments. Emphasize the importance of following safety guidelines, staying with the group, and notifying adults about any concerns.

4. Celebrate Responsible Actions:

- Acknowledge and celebrate instances where kids demonstrate responsible behavior in outdoor settings. Positive reinforcement reinforces the importance of taking safety seriously.

5. Provide Opportunities for Leadership:

- Offer opportunities for kids to take on leadership roles in outdoor activities. This may include leading a short hike, taking charge of a group task, or assisting with setting up camp. Leadership experiences build confidence and a sense of responsibility.

6. Include Them in Planning:

- Involve kids in the planning process for outdoor activities. Discuss safety measures, emergency procedures, and the importance of preparedness. This inclusion reinforces their role in ensuring a safe and enjoyable experience.

7. Reassure and Support:

- Emphasize that it's okay to ask for help when needed. Reassure kids that seeking assistance is a responsible action, and they should never hesitate to reach out to trusted adults or emergency services.

8. Teach Self-Awareness:

- Encourage self-awareness by teaching kids to recognize their own limits and capabilities. Knowing when to ask for help or take a break contributes to responsible decision-making.

Role of Educators and Caregivers

Educators and caregivers play a crucial role in preparing kids for emergencies. Here are key responsibilities and strategies for adults guiding children in outdoor settings:

1. Provide Age-Appropriate Information:

- Tailor information to the age and developmental level of the children. Present concepts in a way that is clear, accessible, and not overwhelming.

2. Conduct Regular Drills:

- Organize regular emergency drills to reinforce the steps kids should take in various situations. Drills create a sense of routine and familiarity with emergency procedures.

3. Create Open Communication:

- Foster open communication between adults and kids. Encourage children to express any concerns or ask questions about safety. Addressing their inquiries builds trust and confidence.

4. Model Calm Behavior:

- Adults should model calm and collected behavior in outdoor settings. Children often emulate the reactions of trusted adults, and maintaining composure sets a positive example.

5. Establish Clear Guidelines:

- Clearly communicate guidelines for behavior and safety in outdoor environments. Consistent messaging reinforces expectations and helps children internalize responsible practices.

6. Provide Adequate Supervision:

- Ensure adequate supervision during outdoor activities. The presence of attentive adults enhances safety and allows for quick response in case of emergencies.

7. Encourage Teamwork:

- Promote a sense of teamwork among children. Encourage them to look out for one another and communicate effectively within the group.

8. Review and Update Information:

- Regularly review and update information about emergency procedures. This ensures that children are aware of the latest guidelines and any changes in protocols.

Conclusion

Empowering kids with the knowledge and skills to navigate emergency situations not only enhances their safety but also fosters a sense of responsibility, confidence, and resilience. By teaching them the key principles of emergency response, practical steps for calling for help, and instilling a proactive mindset, we equip young adventurers to face challenges in the great outdoors with preparedness and composure. The ability to assess situations, make informed decisions, and seek assistance when needed lays a foundation for a lifetime of safe and enjoyable outdoor experiences. In empowering children for outdoor adventures, we contribute to their growth, self-assurance, and a lasting appreciation for the wonders of the natural world.

Made in the USA
Columbia, SC
10 January 2024